Mats Sundin

KERRY BANKS

GREYSTONE BOOKS
Douglas & McIntyre
Vancouver/Toronto

Text copyright © 1998 by Kerry Banks

98 99 00 01   5 4 3 2 1

Greystone Books
A division of Douglas & McIntyre Ltd.
1615 Venables Street
Vancouver, British Columbia
Canada V5L 2H1

Canadian Cataloguing in Publication Data
Banks, Kerry, 1952–
    Mats Sundin
    (Hockey heroes)
    ISBN 1-55054-642-2

    1. Sundin, Mats—Juvenile literature. 2 Hockey players—Canada—
Biography—Juvenile literature. I. Title. II. Series.
GV848.5.S96B36 1998   j796.962'092   c98-910269-6

Editing by Michael Carroll
Cover and text design by Peter Cocking
Front cover photograph by Dave Sandford/Hockey Hall of Fame
Back cover photograph by Jim McIsaac/Bruce Bennett Studios
Printed and bound in Canada by Friesens
Printed on acid-free paper ∞

Photo credits

Photos by Bruce Bennett Studios:
pp. i (top left), 10, 13, 14, 17, 18, 24, 35, 39: Bruce Bennett
pp. i (center left), 5, 20: John Giamundo
pp. 3, 6, 30: Claus Andersen
p. 9: Mark Hicks
pp. 23, 27: Jean-Yves Michaud
p. 28: Robert Skeoch
pp. 32, 40: Jim McIsaac
p. 44: Robert Laberge

Photos by the Hockey Hall of Fame:
pp. i (bottom left, right), iii, iv, 36, 42, 43: Dave Sandford
p. 31: Doug MacLellan

The publisher gratefully acknowledges the assistance of the Canada Council for the Arts and of the British Columbia Ministry of Tourism, Small Business and Culture. The publisher also acknowledges the financial support of the Government of Canada through the Book Publishing Industry Development Program for its publishing activities.

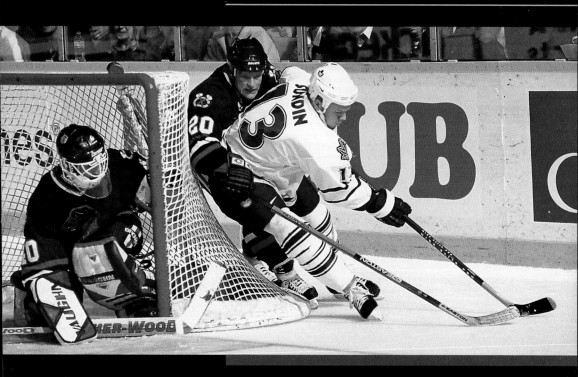

CONTENTS

Speed and power are

the keys to Mats's game.

The Swede's big reach and

long, ice-eating strides

make him a tough player

to defend against.

CHAPTER ONE

The Big Viking

There are only two *S*'s in Mats Sundin's name. But people who know hockey say the Toronto Maple Leaf is a five-*S* player. He has the five ingredients you need to be a superstar in the National Hockey League (NHL): size, strength, speed, skill and spirit. These qualities make Mats a complete player.

At six feet four inches (1.95 meters) and 225 pounds (102 kilograms), Mats is big enough to overpower other players. And his skating speed allows him to outrace opponents trying to check him.

Some people call his speed deceptive. His long, smooth, ice-eating strides allow him to cover in two strokes what other skaters do in three or four. But NHL players who compete against him don't all agree with that description. Trevor Linden of the New York Islanders, who is often given the tough job of shutting down Mats, says, "His speed may look deceptive from up in the press box, but you don't think that down on the ice. I just try to be as physical as I can against him, get in his way, throw him off stride. If you let him get a step on you, he's gone."

Defenseman Nicklas Lidstrom of the Detroit Red Wings says that one of the things that makes Mats a star player are his hands: "He has great hands for someone his size. Soft and very quick." By soft, Lidstrom means that Mats can pass, receive and control the puck with a soft touch. It's a hockey skill that is almost impossible to teach, just like one of Mats's other talents—the ability to read the ice.

Mats takes most of the crucial faceoffs for Toronto.

Reading the ice means you can see which way the play is flowing and where the puck is going to end up. If you can do that, then a lot of scoring chances will come your way. On some nights, the puck seems to follow Mats around.

Bob Gainey, the former NHL great and now the general manager of the Dallas Stars, knows a young player can learn a lot by watching Mats Sundin. "The image that comes to my mind," he says, "when I think about Mats Sundin is the sheer joy he has in playing. I can see him skating and see how much he is enjoying the game. That's a very important thing."

Mats brings many other qualities to hockey besides a love of the game. His ability to perform well when the pressure is intense sets him apart from simply very good players. Mats has always played his best when the games mean the most.

He first showed he had what it takes at the 1991 World Championships. At age 20, Mats was one of the youngest players on the Swedish team, but he still played brilliantly. He scored six goals and five assists in his first nine games of the tournament. And the goals he scored were big ones. In Sweden's match against archrival Finland, he scored twice in 15 seconds to earn his team a crucial 4–4 tie.

Going into the final game against the Soviet Union, Mats was tied with Canada's Joe Sakic for the most points in the tournament. But there was more at stake than just the scoring title—the gold medal was up for grabs. If Sweden won, it would capture the gold. If the Soviets won, they would take home the medal.

The Swedes and Soviets were tied 1–1 with 10 minutes left in the third period. Then Mats picked up the puck and rushed down the ice. With blinding quickness, he deked legendary defenseman Viacheslav Fetisov, burst into the clear and fired the puck into the Soviet net.

The Swedish Connection

Although defenseman Borje Salming was the first Swedish-trained player to have a major impact in the NHL, he wasn't the first of his countrymen to cross the Atlantic Ocean. The first Swedish-trained player to suit up with an NHL team was left winger Ulf Sterner, who had a four-game stint with the New York Rangers in 1964–65. The first Swedish import to play a full NHL season was defenseman Thommie Bergman. He appeared in 75 games with the Detroit Red Wings in 1972–73.

Mats's goal proved to be the winner as Sweden hung on for a 2–1 victory. Afterward, a joyful Mats declared, "That's the most important goal of my career. I can't describe what it feels like. To play for your country really gets you up. What a feeling!"

When the Swedish team returned home, 100,000 fans were waiting to greet it. The biggest cheers were for Mats, the player Swedish sportswriters had nicknamed "Sudden" because of his ability to do the unexpected.

Wearing the blue-and-yellow uniform of the Swedish national team had been Mats's dream since he was a little boy growing up in a suburb of Stockholm. Hockey was a passion in the Sundin family. Mats's father, Tommy, a telephone company planner, was a goalie who once had a tryout with the Swedish national junior team. Mats's older brother, Patrick, and his younger brother, Per, both played hockey, too. Sometimes their father would put on the pads and let his three sons fire pucks at him.

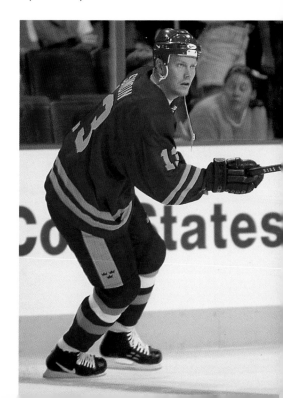

Mats learned to skate at age five on a nearby pond. His first skates were homemade. He simply strapped two blades around each shoe and tied them in place with a strap. At age seven, he went to a hockey school to learn how to play the game. In Sweden this is the first thing a kid does when he wants to

play organized hockey. Unlike most North American children, Mats played all of his games in outdoor rinks. Sweden has only 246 covered arenas compared to 3,000 in Canada and 1,200 in the United States.

Even though Mats followed North American hockey, his major interest was the European game. But he started paying more attention to the NHL when Swedish players began entering the league in the early 1970s.

One of Mats's fondest childhood hockey memories involved former Toronto Maple Leaf defenseman Borje Salming, the first Swedish star in the NHL. In 1976 Salming played for Sweden at the Canada Cup. "All of my friends and family," Mats admits, "remember how wonderful it was to see Borje receive a great ovation from the Maple Leaf Gardens crowd at the 1976 Canada Cup. At that point, we truly realized the impact that Borje had made on the people of Toronto."

Although Mats loved hockey, it wasn't the only sport he played as a boy. He also took part in tennis, soccer, golf and waterskiing. Another game he played was bandy. A European

THE MATS SUNDIN FILE

Position: Center, right wing

Born: February 13, 1971, Bromma, Sweden

Height: Six feet four inches (1.95 meters)

Weight: 225 pounds (102 kilograms)

Shoots: Right

Number: 13

Nickname: The Big Viking

Favorite Rock Band: U2

Favorite Actor: Robert De Niro

Off-Season Hobbies: Golf, fishing

Childhood Hockey Heroes: Kent Nilsson, Mats Naslund

Hockey Highlight: Winning the 1991 World Championships

winter sport similar to hockey, it is played outdoors on huge rinks with a small orange ball.

"Everything that was fun I did until I was 17," Mats says. "I think that's a big reason I was able to choose hockey and still think it was fun. I think a lot of kids nowadays are pushed into a sport by their parents and that they focus on that sport too much at too early an age. Then, when the kids are 18 or 19 years old, they're so sick of the sport they do something else."

The thing Mats most liked about hockey was the friendships he made with his fellow players: "I enjoyed everything about being on the team, from traveling with 20 or 25 guys, to the laughs in the dressing room. To me it doesn't matter if you're seven or 27 years old. The fun part of being on a team stays the same."

Mats doesn't shy away from the rough stuff.

When Mats graduated from high school, he thought about becoming an electrician. First, though, he wanted to see how far he could go in hockey. At 17 his hopes got a boost when he made the Nacka team in the Swedish First Division. Nacka was a farm team where the young players of the Djurgarden club in the Swedish Elite League gained more experience.

Mats only scored 10 goals and eight assists in 25 games with Nacka and wasn't chosen for the Swedish national junior squad. Still, he made a favorable impression on some very important spectators. Up in the stands, NHL scouts were watching his every move.

At age 19, Mats began

his NHL career with a

bang, scoring a goal in

his first game with the

Quebec Nordiques.

C H A P T E R   T W O

Becoming a Pro

On June 17, 1989, Mats Sundin
arrived at the Met Center in
Bloomington, Minnesota, for the biggest day of his young life—
the annual NHL Entry Draft. Until a week before, Mats didn't
even know what the draft was. "I knew they were picking
players," he says, "but I had no clue how it worked."

Eighteen-year-old Mats wasn't prepared for all the attention
the event generated. Making his way through the crowd for a
photo session, he was repeatedly asked to sign autographs. This
was a surprise. No one had ever wanted his autograph before.

The Quebec Nordiques (now the Colorado Avalanche) owned the first pick in the draft. It was expected the Nordiques would use it to select Dave Chyzowski, the top-ranked Canadian junior. He was a left winger who had scored 56 goals with the Kamloops Blazers of the Western Hockey League (WHL). Not much was known about Mats in the NHL. Even most Swedes didn't consider him the top young player in his home country. In fact, he had yet to play a single game in Sweden's Elite League.

But Quebec's scouts liked Mats's skating ability, quick hands, puck sense—and his size. He was six feet three inches (1.92 meters) and weighed 185 pounds (84 kilograms), and he was still growing. Even if Mats was still several years away from making the NHL, the Quebec scouts felt he had the most potential of any player available.

The suspense ended when Pierre Gauthier, the Nordiques' director of scouting, announced, "The Quebec Nordiques select Mats Sundin." It was a historic moment. No European player had ever been chosen first in the draft.

Mats was the first pick at the 1989 NHL Entry Draft.

Mats returned home to play with Djurgarden of the Swedish Elite League in 1989–90, scoring 10 goals and eight assists in 34 games. After the season, he was picked to play on the Swedish national teams at both the World Junior tournament and the World Championships. It should have been an exciting time for the teenager, but all was not well.

A month before the NHL Entry Draft, Djurgarden had pressured Mats into agreeing to a contract. He signed a four-year deal worth about $750 a month without the help of an agent or adviser. Now, with his value suddenly soaring, Mats realized he had made a mistake in signing the contract. So he began a messy battle to get out of it. The move made many Swedes angry. The Swedish media called Mats a traitor. Djurgarden officials threatened to have him banned from international hockey forever if he left. To this day, Mats calls it the worst time of his life.

Eventually Quebec bought out Mats's Djurgarden contract for $300,000. As the details of the deal were hammered out, Gauthier whisked Mats out of Stockholm in disguise. He brought the young Swede to Quebec City and hid him in his home for three days. Then, finally, it was announced that Mats was officially a member of the Nordiques.

Any doubts about Mats's worth soon vanished once he joined the Nordiques. In his first exhibition game in Quebec's arena, the 19-year-old received a tremendous cheer after a dazzling end-to-end rush. In his second preseason game, he scored a goal and set up three others. When the Nordiques opened

Streaky Scorers

Only three players in NHL history—Wayne Gretzky, Mario Lemieux and Mats Sundin—have managed to score a point in 30 or more straight games. Gretzky did it three times with the Edmonton Oilers during the 1980s, achieving 51-, 39- and 30-game point streaks. Lemieux had a 46-game streak with the Pittsburgh Penguins in 1989–90. Sundin put together a 30-game point streak with the Quebec Nordiques in 1992–93. During those 30 games, he scored 21 goals and 25 assists.

their season against the Hartford Whalers (now the Carolina Hurricanes), Mats was in the lineup. He wasted no time getting his name on an NHL scoresheet. He scored his first NHL goal in the third period to give Quebec a come-from-behind 3–3 tie.

Mats had heard that Europeans were often given a hard time in the NHL. Many North American players felt that Europeans were taking jobs away from them. But Mats was welcomed by his teammates. Among them was Guy Lafleur, who was playing the final season of his legendary 17-year NHL career.

However, something else Mats had been told about the NHL proved to be true—the pace of the play. "I couldn't believe how fast it was," he says. "A lot faster than the best league in Sweden and a lot rougher, too."

At first the Nordiques thought Mats should be slowly eased into the lineup. But his play was so impressive that he ended up skating in all 80 games. He recorded 23 goals and 36 assists for 59 points, second on the team to sniper Joe Sakic. Only one other rookie—the Detroit Red Wings' Sergei Fedorov—scored more points.

Mats proved he belonged in the NHL in his rookie year.

The Nordiques were also impressed by Mats's feistiness. Swedish players had an image of being timid, but the baby-faced Sundin didn't disappear when things got tough. "He's in there all the time dishing it out," said Sakic. "He's not afraid of anyone."

What Mats found most difficult about his rookie NHL season was losing. Quebec won only 12 games and finished a

whopping 70 points behind the Boston Bruins, the top team in their division. But getting used to losing wasn't Mats's only challenge. He also had to make some off-ice adjustments. Although he spoke English, he knew no French, the dominant language in Quebec City. This made it hard for him to make new friends. None of the major newspapers were in English, and there was nothing available in Swedish. He also missed the familiar food from his homeland, especially Swedish meatballs. For a kid who had never left home before, it was a lonely experience. In his rookie year, Mats spent $2,000 a month in telephone calls to Sweden.

When the season ended, most of the Nordiques went on vacation, but Mats took a plane to Finland. His hockey season wasn't finished.

SWEDISH SNIPERS

As of 1996–97, only seven Swedish players had scored 40 goals in a single NHL season. Mats Sundin has done it twice. Calgary's Hakan Loob is the only Swede to score 50.

Player	Season	Team	Goals
Hakan Loob	1987–88	Calgary Flames	50
Kent Nilsson	1980–81	Calgary Flames	49
Mats Sundin	1992–93	Quebec Nordiques	47
Kent Nilsson	1982–83	Calgary Flames	46
Tomas Sandstrom	1990–91	Los Angeles Kings	45
Mats Naslund	1985–86	Montreal Canadiens	43
Mats Sundin	1996–97	Toronto Maple Leafs	41

Seizing the spotlight,

Mats scored game-winning

goals for the Swedish

national team in the finals

of the 1991 and 1992

World Championships.

CHAPTER THREE

A National Hero

The players on the Swedish national team noticed a change in Mats when he joined them in Finland for the 1991 World Championships. As defenseman Nicklas Lidstrom recalls, "He looked so much more confident after a year in the NHL. He was really driving to the net. He scored a lot of big goals for us."

The biggest goal was Mats's dramatic game-winner against the Soviet Union, the one that gave Sweden the gold medal. That goal made Mats a national hero. But he had little time to enjoy his new fame. In September he was back on the ice with

Sweden in the Canada Cup. Although Sweden lost in the semifinal to Canada, Mats was Sweden's best player and was voted to the tournament all-star team.

But all that hockey took a toll. When Mats rejoined the Nordiques for the 1992–93 season, his legs simply had no jump. He was burnt out after two training camps, a World Championship, a Canada Cup and an 80-game NHL season packed into only 12 months.

Mats wasn't the only sluggish player in Quebec. The whole team seemed to be sleepwalking, a situation many blamed on what became known as the "the Eric Lindros affair."

Because the Nordiques had finished in last place, they again had the first pick in that summer's NHL Entry Draft. They used it to select Eric Lindros, the most talented Canadian to come out of junior hockey since Mario Lemieux. Lindros was expected to make Quebec a much stronger team. But he didn't want to play for Quebec. He believed he could make more money and become a bigger star if he played for a team in a larger city. The wrangle over his refusal to sign became a huge distraction for the Nordiques.

Mats racked up 114 points for Quebec in 1992–93.

Things began looking up for Mats in February when coach Pierre Pagé moved him to center to replace injured Joe Sakic. In 54 games at right wing, Mats had scored 15 goals. In his last 26 games at center, he scored 18 goals and 36 points, a pace that would have given him 58 goals and 116 points over a full season.

By March 5, as the Nordiques were about to play the Hartford Whalers, they were winless in 33 straight road games. This
was just four games short of the NHL record of 37 straight road
games without a win, set by the Washington Capitals in 1974–75.
But that night against the Whalers, Mats scored a remarkable
five goals and two assists, leading Quebec to a 10–4 victory.

However, the lopsided win was just a brief high for the
struggling Nordiques, who limped home with 52 points. Only
the even worse play of the expansion San Jose Sharks saved
Quebec from finishing last in the NHL for a fourth straight year.

Mats was back with the Swedish national team for the 1992
World Championships in Czechoslovakia. Although he started

slowly in the tournament, he soon
picked up steam. He scored the most
spectacular goal of the championships, an end-to-end rush against
the Soviet Union to spark a 2–0
Swedish victory. He turned in
another powerful game as Sweden
knocked off Finland 5–2 in the
final to claim the gold medal for
the second straight year.

During the off-season, Quebec
traded Eric Lindros to the Phila-
delphia Flyers in exchange for Steve
Duchesne, Kerry Huffman, Mike
Ricci, Ron Hextall, Chris Simon,

Peter Forsberg and the Flyers' first draft pick in 1993 and 1994. Quebec improved immediately, jumping from 20 to 47 wins and posting 104 points in 1992–93. This was good enough for second place in the Adams Division, only five points behind the first-place Boston Bruins.

Surrounded by stronger players, Mats had a terrific year. He began the season with a 30-game point-scoring streak, the longest in the league that year, and the third longest in NHL history. By the end of the season, he had piled up 114 points on 47 goals and 67 assists, the best on the Nordiques.

But the Nordiques' inexperience hurt them in their first-round playoff series with Montreal. They took too many chances offensively, forgot about defensive play and lost to the Canadiens in six games. The series' most memorable image came in the last game when television viewers saw frustrated coach Pierre Pagé verbally attack Mats as he sat glumly on the bench.

Based on their improved showing in 1992–93, Quebec was expected to be a league power in 1993–94. Some hockey experts predicted Mats would reach 120 points. He began the season strongly, scoring 19 goals in his

High Five

Fewer than 30 players in modern NHL history have scored five or more goals in a game. Mats Sundin joined this elite club on March 5, 1992. Playing center on a line with wingers Owen Nolan and Valeri Kamensky, he exploded for five goals and two assists as the Quebec Nordiques beat the Hartford Whalers 10–4. Mats's effort broke the Nordiques' single-game record of four goals, held by Peter Stastny and Michel Goulet. Combined with Nolan's one goal and five assists, and Kamensky's two goals and three assists, Mats's line racked up an amazing 18 points.

first 29 games, and was on pace for a 105-point season. But trouble was brewing behind the scenes.

Mats was unhappy with his contract. He felt he was being underpaid. He was in the third year of a five-year deal that paid him $900,000 a year, far less than the $2.8 million the club was paying Joe Sakic.

Mats believed he had a promise from the team's management that they would renegotiate his contract. But in December, Nordiques president Marcel Aubut said he wouldn't renegotiate the deal. Afterward, Mats slumped badly, scoring just 13 goals in his last 55 games. Instead of having a breakthrough year, the Nordiques missed the playoffs.

After the season, Pierre Pagé was fired. Marc Crawford became the new coach and Pierre Lacroix took over as general manager. Lacroix made it clear he wanted to change the chemistry of his disappointing team. Mats's days with the Nordiques were numbered.

TOOLS OF THE TRADE

Mats Sundin uses an extra-long stick. It measures 63 inches (1.6 meters) from the heel to the top of the shaft, the maximum length allowed by NHL rules. It's tougher to control the puck with a long stick. But Mats's reach allows him to handle it. The advantage of a long stick is that you can shoot the puck harder. At the start of each season, Mats will order 360 new sticks. That may sound like a lot, but during the year, he'll give many of them away at charity events.

As for his other gear, he likes his skates to feel quite stiff and he'll wear them almost brand-new. He might try on a new pair at the team's morning skate and then use them in a game that same night. Many players will wear one pair of skates all season long, but Mats gets a new pair every month.

The blockbuster 1994

trade that sent Mats from

Quebec to Toronto in

exchange for Wendel Clark

was headline news in

both Sweden and Canada.

CHAPTER FOUR

A New Leaf

In June 1994, Mats Sundin was trout fishing in northern Sweden when he was tracked down by Swedish reporters in helicopters. They had come to get his reaction to the big trade.

Quebec had sent Mats, Garth Butcher, Todd Warriner and a first-round draft choice to the Toronto Maple Leafs in return for Wendel Clark, Sylvain Lefebvre, Landon Wilson and a first-round draft choice. The trade created shock waves in Toronto. Clark, the Leafs' captain, had just come off a 46-goal season and was regarded as the leader of the team.

The day after the deal was made, the *Toronto Star* newspaper sent a reporter to the northern Swedish town of Kiruna to interview Mats. He was working there as an instructor at Borje Salming's hockey school. The reporter brought along some Toronto newspapers. As Mats scanned the headlines, he kept repeating, "Oh, boy. Oh, boy." Clearly this wasn't any ordinary hockey trade.

"When you look at what Toronto gave away," Mats said back then, "I understand what is happening. Wendel Clark was a star—a legend. He was the soul of the team. I'm not looking to replace him. That's impossible. We're different types of players. I'll just try to contribute the best way I can."

That contribution had to wait. A labor dispute between the players and the NHL management delayed the opening of the 1994–95 season until January 13. When the games finally did get under way, hockey fans were in a surly mood. Torontonians, already annoyed by the loss of their favorite player, were especially cranky. It wasn't an easy environment for Mats to step into.

He was the target of scattered boos in the Leafs' preseason games. But when he was introduced at the club's home opener versus the Vancouver Canucks on January 25, the fans cheered him warmly. Mats scored a goal and an assist in the Leafs' 6–2 win.

The Leaf team was very different from Quebec's youthful squad. Toronto had reached the Western Conference finals in the past two seasons. The club was loaded with veterans.

SUNDIN VERSUS FORSBERG

When hockey fans debate who is the best Swedish player, it usually comes down to two names: Mats Sundin and Peter Forsberg. Both are heroes in their homeland. Mats scored the winning goal for Sweden at the 1991 World Championships. In 1994 Peter scored the winning goal in a shoot-out to give Sweden its first-ever Olympic gold medal. Mats admits the two have a private rivalry. Whenever his team, the Maple Leafs, plays Peter's team, the Colorado Avalanche, he feels an extra challenge. Says Mats, "The competition is special. It's good for me because it makes me push myself all the time."

Mats was unsure where he would fit in with such proven NHL players as Doug Gilmour, Mike Gartner and Dave Andreychuk.

But it wasn't just the team that was different. Toronto was a much bigger place than Quebec City and the hockey coverage was far more intense. Playing in Toronto was like playing in a fishbowl. Everything that happened to the Leafs was put under a microscope.

Mats led the Leafs in scoring in the shortened 1994–95 season with 47 points in 47 games. But he was still criticized. One of his loudest critics was *Hockey Night in Canada* commentator Don Cherry, who questioned Mats's "heart" on national television. Cherry's favorite players were "grinders"— players who enjoyed slamming and banging and who were fast with their fists. Mats played a smoother, more polished

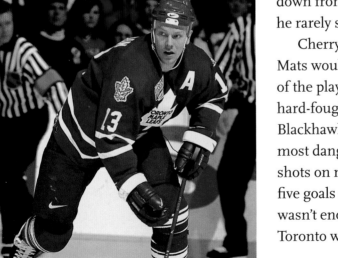

style of game. He didn't back down from physical contact, but he rarely started it.

Cherry and others predicted that Mats would fade in the tough going of the playoffs. But in the Leafs' hard-fought series with the Chicago Blackhawks, Mats was the club's most dangerous threat. He fired 27 shots on net and led the team with five goals and nine points. Still, it wasn't enough to turn the tide, as Toronto went down in seven games.

With one season as a Maple Leaf under his belt, Mats entered the 1995–96 campaign feeling more relaxed and more confident. But he still had to face one more test. On October 10, 1995, the Leafs hosted the New York Islanders. The game marked the first appearance of Wendel Clark at Maple Leaf Gardens since his trade to the Nordiques. Only a week before, the Nordiques, who had moved to Colorado in the off-season, had sent Clark to the Islanders for Claude Lemieux.

Barging around in his typically rambunctious style, Clark twice caused the crowd to explode in cheers before the game was 10 minutes old. Rather than wilt under the pressure, Mats rose to the occasion. He rattled eight shots on net, scoring twice and adding two assists as Toronto romped to a 7–3 win. After jamming in a rebound for the Leafs' first goal, Mats pounded the glass behind the Islanders' net with his fist in a burst of emotion. By the end of the game, the Gardens crowd was cheering Mats and the Leafs.

Positioned for much of the season on right wing with center Doug Gilmour, Mats again led the Leafs in scoring. He racked up 83 points on 33 goals and 50 assists. On December 23, against the Edmonton Oilers, the Big Viking scored a pretty breakaway goal on a pass from Gilmour. It was Gilmour's 1,000th NHL point.

Unlucky Number?

Mats Sundin may have his superstitions, but the fear of number 13 is not one of them. Mats is one of the few NHL players to wear this supposedly unlucky number. As he notes, "I had number 13 when I played as a kid in Sweden. Maybe it's because my birthday is on the 13th of February, but I can't say, because I had the number since I was very young. When I turned professional with the Nordiques, 13 was available, so it was natural to go back to the number I was wearing throughout my childhood."

In mid-season Mats achieved another honor. He was selec-
ted to play in his first NHL All-Star Game. Mats was joined by
three other Swedes: Peter Forsberg of the Colorado Avalanche,
Nicklas Lidstrom of the Detroit Red Wings and Daniel
Alfredsson of the Ottawa Senators. But the thrill of playing
in the All-Star Game was soon forgotten when the Leafs fell
into a terrible slump that caused head coach Pat Burns to
be fired and replaced by Nick Beverley.

In March the Leafs made two deals in a bid to turn things
around. They sent Dave Andreychuk to the New Jersey Devils
and reacquired Wendel Clark from the Islanders. But the trades
didn't help. Toronto finished 13th overall and third in their
division with 80 points. And any hopes of a comeback in the
postseason were quickly shattered as the Leafs were bounced
out of the playoffs in the first round by the St. Louis Blues.

Mats has appeared

in three straight

NHL All-Star Games.

The 1995–96 season was a very good one
for Mats. He scored 83 points on 33 goals and 50
assists, tops on the Leafs. But Toronto's quick
playoff exit and the continuing criticism of Mats's
play left a bitter taste. That summer he decided
to do something about it. Mats began a weight-
training program. He worked out five times
a week and added 15 pounds (6.8 kilograms) of muscle, most
of it in his legs and lower body.

Hockey fans would get their first look at the bigger and
improved Mats Sundin in September at the eight-nation World
Cup tournament. It proved to be an eyeful.

Because Mats is Toronto's

most dangerous scorer,

opposing teams usually

give their best checkers the

task of shutting him down.

C H A P T E R   F I V E

Toronto Tornado

There were two headline stories at the 1996 World Cup. One was Team USA's upset of Team Canada in the tournament final. The other was the sizzling performance of Mats Sundin. Although he played only four games, he was the third-leading scorer in the tournament with seven points. In Sweden's double-overtime thriller against Canada in the semifinals, he set up the third-period goal that forced sudden death, had 10 shots on goal and caused headaches for the Canadian team with his whirlwind rushes.

"It's the best I've ever seen Sundin play and I don't think he ever got tired," said Canadian coach Glen Sather. "He was the one guy on the ice who did not slow down. We had to have someone on him at all times. If we didn't, he would have killed us."

Swedish coach Kent Forsberg said, "He was the star of the tournament. I expected him to be good, but he was great. He has never played better. He played both ends of the ice. He forechecked, backchecked. He did it all."

Being the top player in a game is one thing, but to dominate against the world's best is something else entirely. It was the high point in Mats's career and it opened a lot of people's eyes to his true abilities.

Mats was pleased with his play and the compliments he received. He credited his awesome performance to his off-season exercise program. Bulked up to 225 pounds (102 kilograms), he may have lost a bit of open-ice speed, but the extra muscle he added to his lower body paid off. It gave him better balance on his skates, greater stamina and the power needed to fight through checks and hold off opponents when breaking in on net.

Using his World Cup momentum, Mats got off to a fast start in 1996–97 under new Leaf head coach Mike Murphy. He recorded a nine-game and an 11-game

Heavy Medal

Mats Sundin has played for Sweden in four World Championships, a Canada Cup, a World Cup and an Olympics. His total medal haul? Three golds, one silver and two bronzes. In the seven tournaments, Mats led the Swedish team in scoring five times. The only times he didn't were at the 1990 World Championships and at the 1998 Olympics.

point streak in the first three months of the season. By the end of the season, he had 41 goals and 53 assists for 94 points, the seventh-highest total in the NHL. But while his play soared, the Leafs sputtered.

In a move to cut costs, the team had shipped out veterans Mike Gartner, Dave Gagner and Todd Gill. But there were no young players ready to take up the slack. The last step in the dismantling of the club's old core came on February 25.

Captain Doug Gilmour was traded to the New Jersey Devils along with defenseman Dave Ellett for three young prospects. Toronto finished last in their division and 23rd overall.

Prior to the opening of the 1997–98 season, Toronto decided to make major changes in its front office. The Leafs dismissed president and general manager Cliff Fletcher and replaced him with former Montreal Canadien goalie great Ken Dryden. One of Dryden's first moves was to pick a new team captain.

After careful thought, he gave the C to Mats Sundin. There was no disguising Mats's delight. At the press conference to announce his appointment, the 26-year-old wore a huge smile. "This is such a thrill. Even though I'm from Europe, I know what being captain of the Toronto Maple Leafs means. It's a big honor and a big responsibility."

In fact, after being told he was going to be given the captaincy the night before at a team dinner, Mats immediately phoned home to give his family the news. "I woke everybody up. It was 6.00 A.M. their time."

Coach Mike Murphy, who recommended that Mats be given the C, noted: "I think it's important for Mats to realize the potential he has both as a player and a leader. He should be the spokesman for our team because he's our pivotal player. There's not one crucial situation I don't put Mats in, whether it's a key faceoff, a power play or a five-on-three penalty kill."

Number 13 is tough to stop once he's in full flight.

As the 1997–98 season progressed, it was clear that Toronto still had a long way to go before it could be ranked as a Stanley

Cup contender. The young club simply lacked offensive firepower. Opposing teams routinely focused on Mats. They figured if they could shut him down, they would win the game. On many nights that was the case.

Because the expectations Toronto fans put on Mats are so high, he is still sometimes blamed for not doing enough. *Toronto Star* sportswriter Paul Hunter, who has seen Mats play a

lot of hockey in a Maple Leaf uniform, thinks that's a bad rap. "Sundin carries the team most nights. He plays 25 minutes, takes a regular turn on the power play and kills penalties. You can count on him doing something spectacular every few games, something that leaves you shaking your head. He's an outstanding player. Mats's problem is that he's never had especially skilled players on the Leafs to complement him. As we saw in the World Cup, if you surround him with skilled players, then there's no ceiling to his game."

Despite his team's struggles, Mats continues to think positively. He says he enjoys living in Toronto and being part of a first-class organization like the Maple Leafs. Even though the frustrations of playing on a losing team sometimes get him down, he knows there are far worse places than where he is now.

"If I'm going through a hard part of my life, I just think about the fact I am living my dream. A lot of people aren't as fortunate to have their hobby—the thing they love to do most—as their job. I just think about that and I feel better."

C STANDS FOR CAPTAIN

On September 30, 1997, Mats Sundin became the 16th captain in the long and celebrated history of the Toronto Maple Leafs. His name joined the ranks of such famous former Leaf captains as Syl Apps, Ted Kennedy, George Armstrong, Dave Keon and Darryl Sittler. But the honor was doubly important for Mats, because it broke an un-spoken barrier. For the first time, the Maple Leaf C no longer stood strictly for Canadian.

It was a sign that the old biases against Euro-pean players were falling by the wayside.

Mats was keenly aware of the significance of the letter stitched onto his jersey. "It shows that you can be from anywhere and still be part of the leadership of an NHL team. This is something that would have been impossible 10 to 15 years ago. It's nice to see that Toronto and the league nowadays are a mix of players from all over the world."

STATISTICS

National Hockey League (NHL)

Regular Season

Year	Team	GP	G	A	P	PIM
1990–91	Quebec	80	23	36	59	58
1991–92	Quebec	80	33	43	76	105
1992–93	Quebec	80	47	67	114	96
1993–94	Quebec	84	32	53	85	60
1994–95	Toronto	47	23	24	47	14
1995–96	Toronto	76	33	50	83	46
1996–97	Toronto	82	41	53	94	59
1997–98	Toronto	74	29	36	65	45
Totals		**603**	**261**	**362**	**623**	**481**

Playoffs

Year	Team	GP	G	A	P	PIM
1991	Quebec	Did Not Qualify				
1992	Quebec	Did Not Qualify				
1993	Quebec	6	3	1	4	6
1994	Quebec	Did Not Qualify				
1995	Toronto	7	5	4	9	4
1996	Toronto	6	3	1	4	4
1997	Toronto	Did Not Qualify				
1998	Toronto	Did Not Qualify				
Totals		**19**	**11**	**6**	**17**	**14**

Swedish Leagues

Regular Season

Year	Team	GP	G	A	P	PIM
1988–89	Nacka	25	10	8	18	18
1989–90	Djurgarden	34	10	8	18	16
1994–95	Djurgarden	12	7	2	9	14
Totals		**71**	**27**	**18**	**45**	**48**

Playoffs

Year	Team	GP	G	A	P	PIM
1990	Djurgarden	8	7	0	7	4

Swedish International Hockey

Year	Event	GP	G	A	P	PIM
1990	World Championships	4	0	0	0	0
1991	World Championships	10	7	5	12	12
1991	Canada Cup	6	2	4	6	16
1992	World Championships	8	2	6	8	8
1994	World Championships	8	5	9	14	6
1996	World Cup	4	4	3	7	4
1998	Olympics	4	3	0	3	4
1998	World Championships	10	5	6	11	2
Totals		**54**	**28**	**33**	**61**	**52**

Key

GP = Games Played   G = Goals   A = Assists
P = Points   PIM = Penalties in Minutes